P9-AQZ-225

99 Tortuous, Tricky, Tough, Tongue Twisters

JOHN JESTER

Copyright © 2014 John Jester
All rights reserved.

99 Tortuous, tricky, tough tongue twisters to keep you amused for hours.

Challenge yourself and your friends to see who really is the tongue twister champion.

Includes the

'World's Hardest Tongue Twister', as researched by psychologists at MIT.

Not only are you guaranteed fun and laughter, but tongue twisters have been proven to improve English pronunciation skills too, for both native speakers and foreign language students.

Freshly-fried flying fish,
freshly-fried flesh.
Freshly-fried flying fish,
freshly-fried flesh.
Freshly-fried flying fish,
freshly-fried flesh.

Which witch wished which
wicked wish?
Which witch wished which
wicked wish?
Which witch wished which
wicked wish?

Yellow yo-yos.
Yellow yo-yos.
Yellow yo-yos.

Sister Suzie's sewing socks
for soldiers
Socks for soldiers sister
Suzie sews,
If sister Suzie's sewing socks
for soldiers,
Where're the socks for soldiers
sister Suzie sews?

If a noisy noise annoys an onion,
an annoying noisy noise annoys
an onion more!

The gum glue grew glum.
The gum glue grew glum.
The gum glue grew glum.

One smart fellow; he felt smart.
Two smart fellows; they
felt smart.
Three smart fellows; they all
felt smart.

Three free throws.
Three free throws.
Three free throws.

Frogfeet, flippers, swimfins.
Frogfeet, flippers, swimfins.
Frogfeet, flippers, swimfins.

Mrs. Smith's fish sauce shop.
Mrs. Smith's fish sauce shop.
Mrs. Smith's fish sauce shop.

Red leather, yellow leather.
Red leather, yellow leather.
Red leather, yellow leather.

Knapsack straps.
Knapsack straps.
Knapsack straps.

Upper roller, lower roller.
Upper roller, lower roller.
Upper roller, lower roller.

Crisp crusts crackle crunchily.
Crisp crusts crackle crunchily.
Crisp crusts crackle crunchily.

A bitter biting bittern
Bit a better brother bittern,
And the bitter better bittern
Bit the bitter biter back.
And the bitter bittern, bitten,
By the better bitten bittern,
Said: "I'm a bitter biter bit,
alack!"

Peggy Babcock.
Peggy Babcock.
Peggy Babcock.

Chipp couldn't chop chocolate
chips 'cause Chip chipped his
chocolate chip chopper.

Mr. See owned a saw.
And Mr. Soar owned a see-saw.
Now, See's saw sawed Soar's
see-saw
Before Soar saw See,
Which made Soar sore.
Had Soar seen See's saw
Before See sawed Soar's
see-saw,
See's saw would not have sawed
Soar's see-saw.
So See's saw sawed Soar's
see-saw.
But it was sad to see Soar
so sore
just because See's saw sawed
Soar's see-saw.

The sixth sick sheik's sixth
sheep's sick.
The sixth sick sheik's sixth
sheep's sick.
The sixth sick sheik's sixth
sheep's sick.

A cup of proper coffee in a
copper coffee cup.
A cup of proper coffee in a
copper coffee cup.
A cup of proper coffee in a
copper coffee cup.

Mix, Miss Mix!
Mix, Miss Mix!
Mix, Miss Mix!

Three sweet switched Swiss
witches watch three washed Swiss
witch Swatch watch switches.
Which sweet switched Swiss
witch watches which washed
Swiss witch Swatch watch switch?

Linda-Lou Lambert loves
lemon lollipop lip gloss.
Linda-Lou Lambert loves
lemon lollipop lip gloss.
Linda-Lou Lambert loves
lemon lollipop lip gloss.

On a nutty knotty knocker
is a noisy niecy nutty knotty
knocker knock.

Six thick thistle sticks.
Six thick thistles sticks.
Six thick thistle sticks.
Six thick thistles sticks.
Six thick thistle sticks.
Six thick thistles sticks.

Double bubble gum
bubbles double.
Double bubble gum
bubbles double.
Double bubble gum
bubbles double

Shredded Swiss cheese.
Shredded Swiss cheese.
Shredded Swiss cheese.

Noisy knobbly-kneed gnome
Had nine nice nieces
Who knocked nine times,
On a nutty knotty knocker.
The nine nice nieces were known
to be naughty,
For eighty-one knocks

Pete, please pass the
plate of peas.
Pete, please pass the
plate of peas.
Pete, please pass the
plate of peas

Silly snowman slides and slips.
Silly snowman slides and slips.
Silly snowman slides and slips.

Sixty-six sick chicks are stuck
in the stock room full of
sixty-six sticks.
Sixty-six sick chicks are stuck
in the stock room full of
sixty-six sticks.
Sixty-six sick chicks are stuck
in the stock room full of
sixty six-sticks.

A good cook could cook good!
A good cook could cook good!
A good cook could cook good!

Baboon bamboo.
Baboon bamboo.
Baboon bamboo.

No nose knows like a
gnome's nose knows.
No nose knows like a
gnome's nose knows.
No nose knows like a
gnome's nose knows.

Around the rugged rocks the
ragged rascals ran.
Around the rugged rocks the
ragged rascals ran.
Around the rugged rocks the
ragged rascals ran.

Daddy draws doors.
Daddy draws doors.
Daddy draws doors.

Of all the felt I ever felt,
I never felt a piece of felt
Which felt as fine as that
felt felt,
When first I felt that felt
hat's felt.

Can you can a canned can into
an uncanned can like a canner
can can a canned can into an
uncanned can?

Bubble bobble.
Bubble bobble.
Bubble bobble.

The myth of Miss Muffet.
The myth of Miss Muffet.
The myth of Miss Muffet.

Jumping Jacky jeered a
jesting juggler.
Did Jumping Jacky jeer a
jesting juggler?
If Jumping Jacky jeered a
jesting juggler,
Then where is the jesting juggler
that Jumping Jacky jeered?

Unique New York.
Unique New York.
Unique New York.

If one doctor doctors another doctor, does the doctor who doctors the doctor doctor the doctor the way the doctor he is doctoring doctors? Or does he doctor the doctor the way the doctor who doctors doctors?

The cheeky chief chef chicken chatted to the second chef chicken as he cooked.
The cheeky chief chef chicken chatted to the second chef chicken as he cooked.
The cheeky chief chef chicken chatted to the second chef chicken as he cooked.

Girl gargoyle, guy gargoyle.
Girl gargoyle, guy gargoyle.
Girl gargoyle, guy gargoyle.

I need not your needles, they're
needless to me;
For kneading of noodles, 'twere
needless, you see;
But did my neat knickers but
need to be kneed,
I then should have need of your
needles indeed.

Cheap ship trip.
Cheap ship trip.
Cheap ship trip

Purple paper people.
Purple paper people.
Purple paper people.

Denise sees the fleece,
Denise sees the fleas.
At least Denise could sneeze
and feed and freeze the fleas.

Ought the tutor get hot
If the Hottentot tot
Hoot and toot at her
Hottentot tutor?

The blue bluebird blinks.
The blue bluebird blinks.
The blue bluebird blinks.

A canner can can anything
that he can,
but a canner can't can
a can, can he?
A canner can can anything
that he can,
but a canner can't can
a can, can he?
A canner can can anything
that he can,
but a canner can't can a can,
can he?

Good blood, bad blood.
Good blood, bad blood.
Good blood, bad blood.

If a Hottentot taught a
Hottentot tot
To talk ere the tot could totter,
Ought the Hottenton tot
Be taught to say aught,
or naught,
Or what ought to be taught her?
If to hoot and to toot a
Hottentot tot
Be taught by her
Hottentot tutor,

Silly Sally swiftly shooed
seven silly sheep.
The seven silly sheep
Silly Sally shooed
Shilly-shallied south.
These sheep shouldn't
sleep in a shack;
Sheep should sleep in a shed.

Will you, William?
Will you, William?
Will you, William?

One black beetle bled
only black blood,
the other black beetle bled blue.
One black beetle bled
only black blood,
the other black beetle bled blue.
One black beetle bled
only black blood,
the other black beetle bled blue.

Greek grapes.
Greek grapes.
Greek grapes.

Lesser leather never weathered
wetter weather better.
Lesser leather never weathered
wetter weather better.
Lesser leather never weathered
wetter weather better.

Six slim slick sycamore saplings.
Six slim slick sycamore saplings.
Six slim slick sycamore saplings.

Old oily Ollie oils old oily autos.
Old oily Ollie oils old oily autos.
Old oily Ollie oils old oily autos.

Friendly fleas and fireflies.
Friendly fleas and fireflies
Friendly fleas and fireflies.

Betty Botter had some butter,
"But," she said,
"this butter's bitter.
If I bake this bitter butter,
It would make my batter bitter.
But a bit of better butter,
That would make my
batter better."
So she bought a bit of butter –
Better than her bitter butter –
And she baked it in her batter;
And the batter was not bitter.
So 'twas better Betty Botter
Bought a bit of better butter.

Rush the washing, Russel.
Rush the washing, Russel.
Rush the washing, Russel.

Many an anemone sees an
enemy anemone.
Many an anemone sees an
enemy anemone.
Many an anemone sees an
enemy anemone.

Six slippery snails, slid
slowly seaward.
Six slippery snails, slid
slowly seaward.
Six slippery snails, slid
slowly seaward.

But if the shot Shott shot
shot Shott,
Then Shott was shot, not Nott.
However, the shot Shott shot
shot not Shott, but Nott.

Eleven owls licked eleven little
liquorice lollipops.
Eleven owls licked eleven little
liquorice lollipops.
Eleven owls licked eleven little
liquorice lollipops.

I wish to wish the wish you wish
to wish, but if you wish the wish
the witch wishes, I won't wish the
wish you wish to wish.

Sam's shop stocks short
spotted socks.
Sam's shop stocks short
spotted socks.
Sam's shop stocks short
spotted socks.

Ned Nott was shot and Sam
Shott was not.
So it is better to be Shott
than Nott.
Some say Nott was not shot.
But Shott says he shot Nott.
Either the shot Shott shot at
Nott was not shot,
Or Nott was shot.
If the shot Shott shot shot Nott,
Nott was shot.

Fred fed Ted bread, and Ted
fed Fred bread.
Fred fed Ted bread, and Ted
fed Fred bread.
Fred fed Ted bread, and Ted
fed Fred bread

When a twister a-twisting will
twist him a twist,
For the twisting a twist, he three
twines will entwist;
But if one of the twines of the
twist do untwist,
The twine that untwisteth
untwisteth the twist.

Sure the ship's shipshape, sir.
Sure the ship's shipshape, sir.
Sure the ship's shipshape, sir.

Susan shineth shoes and socks;
Socks and shoes shines Susan.
She ceases shining shoes
and socks,
For shoes and socks
shock Susan.

The big bug bit the little beetle,
but the little beetle bit the big
bug back.
The big bug bit the little beetle,
but the little beetle bit the big
bug back.
The big bug bit the little beetle,
but the little beetle bit the big
bug back.

Bad money, mad bunny.
Bad money, mad bunny.
Bad money, mad bunny.

Whistle for the thistle sifter.
Whistle for the thistle sifter.
Whistle for the thistle sifter.

Imagine an imaginary
menagerie manager
imagining managing an
imaginary menagerie.
Imagine an imaginary
menagerie manager
imagining managing an
imaginary menagerie.
Imagine an imaginary
menagerie manager
imagining managing an
imaginary menagerie.

Nine nice night nurses
nursing nicely.
Nine nice night nurses
nursing nicely.
Nine nice night nurses
nursing nicely.

A skunk sat on a stump and thunk the stump stunk, but the stump thunk the skunk stunk.
A skunk sat on a stump and thunk the stump stunk, but the stump thunk the skunk stunk.
A skunk sat on a stump and thunk the stump stunk, but the stump thunk the skunk stunk.

A bloke's back bike brake block broke.
A bloke's back bike brake block broke.
A bloke's back bike brake block broke.

A tutor who tooted the flute
Tried to tutor two tooters
to toot.
Said the two to the tutor:
"Is it harder to toot or
To tutor two tooters to toot?"

Thieves seize skis.
Thieves seize skis.
Thieves seize skis.

The instinct of an extinct
insect stinks.
The instinct of an extinct
insect stinks.
The instinct of an extinct
insect stinks.

A tree-toad loved a she-toad
Who lived up in a tree.
He was a two-toed tree-toad,
But a three-toed toad was she.
The two-toed tree-toad
tried to win
The three-toed she-toad's heart,
For the two-toed tree-toad
loved the ground
That the three-toed
tree-toad trod.
But the two-toed tree-toad
tried in vain;
He couldn't please her whim.
From her tree-toad bower,
With her three-toed power,
The she-toad vetoed him.

Penny's pretty pink piggy bank.
Penny's pretty pink piggy bank.
Penny's pretty pink piggy bank.

Ed had edited it.
Ed had edited it.
Ed had edited it.

Rubber baby buggy bumpers.
Rubber baby buggy bumpers.
Rubber baby buggy bumpers.

Six sharp smart sharks.
Six sharp smart sharks.
Six sharp smart sharks.

Brad's big black
bath brush broke.
Brad's big black
bath brush broke.
Brad's big black
bath brush broke.

You've no need to light
a night-light
On a light night like tonight,
For a night-light's light's
a slight light,
And tonight's a night
that's light.
When a night's light, like
tonight's light,
It is really not quite right
To light night-lights with their
slight lights
On a light night like tonight.

Listen to the local yokel yodel.
Listen to the local yokel yodel.
Listen to the local yokel yodel.

Chop shops stock chops.
Chop shops stock chops.
Chop shops stock chops.

Irish wristwatch.
Irish wristwatch.
Irish wristwatch.

Sixish.
Sixish.
Sixish.

Sly Sam slurps Sally's soup.
Sly Sam slurps Sally's soup.
Sly Sam slurps Sally's soup.

Give Mr. Snipa's wife's
knife a swipe.
Give Mr. Snipa's wife's
knife a swipe.
Give Mr. Snipa's wife's
knife a swipe.

A sweet and well-swum swan
swam swimmingly.
A sweet and well-swum swan
swam swimmingly.
A sweet and well-swum swan
swam swimmingly.

The quick-witted cricket
critic quit.
The quick-witted cricket
critic quit.
The quick-witted cricket
critic quit.

Five frantic frogs fled from fifty
fierce fishes.
Five frantic frogs fled from fifty
fierce fishes.
Five frantic frogs fled from fifty
fierce fishes.

And finally, the one you have been waiting for. Devised by the psychologists at MIT, this is supposed to be the hardest tongue twister of them all.

Good luck.

Pad kid poured curd pulled cold.
Pad kid poured curd pulled cold.
Pad kid poured curd pulled cold.
Pad kid poured curd pulled cold.
Pad kid poured curd pulled cold.
Pad kid poured curd pulled cold.
Pad kid poured curd pulled cold.
Pad kid poured curd pulled cold.
Pad kid poured curd pulled cold.
Pad kid poured curd pulled cold.

Made in the USA
Columbia, SC
17 March 2021

34654969R00024